Empowered IN HIM

Study Guide

Peta Taberner

Empowered IN HIM Study Guide
First published by Bekker Media for Hope Ministries International 2025
www. hopeministriesinternational.com.au

All rights reserved. Without limiting the rights under copyright reserved above, no part of this publication may be reproduced, stored in or introduced into a database and retrieval system or transmitted in any form or any means (electronic, mechanical, photocopying, recording or otherwise) without the prior written permission of both the owner of the copyright and the above publishers. The only exception is brief quotations in printed reviews.

Printed by IngramSpark in 2025
ISBN: 978-0-9756199-2-6

Unless otherwise specified, all scripture taken from the New King James Version®. Copyright © 1982 by Thomas Nelson. Used by permission. All rights reserved.

Scripture quotations marked NLT are taken from the Holy Bible, New Living Translation. Copyright © 1996, 2004, 2015 by Tyndale House Foundation. Used by permission of Tyndale House Ministries, Carol Stream, Illinois 60188. All rights reserved.

Scripture quotations marked TPT are taken from The Passion Translation®. Copyright © 2017, 2018 by Passion & Fire Ministries, Inc. Used by permission. All rights reserved. ThePassionTranslation.com.

Scripture quotations taken from the Amplified® Bible (AMP), Copyright © 2015 by The Lockman Foundation. Used by permission.

The Holy Bible, Berean Standard Bible, BSB is produced in cooperation with Bible Hub, Discovery Bible, OpenBible.com, and the Berean Bible Translation Committee. This text of God's Word has been dedicated to the public domain.

CONTENTS

INTRODUCTION — 5

1 INTIMACY - RELATIONSHIP WITH JESUS — 9
— Questions
— Reflection

2 OUR IDENTITY — 19
— Questions
— Reflection

3 BALANCING MINISTRY AND FAMILY — 31
— Questions
— Reflection

4 FIVE-FOLD GIFTS — 37
— What are the five-fold gifts?
— Apostle - the apostle governs
— Prophet - the prophet guides
— Pastor - the pastor guards
— Evangelist - the evangelist gathers
— Teacher - the teacher grounds
— Reflection

5 ADDITIONAL SPIRITUAL GIFTS — 59
— How Do I Know What My Spiritual Gifts Are?
— Question
— Reflection

6 EQUIPPED AND EMPOWERED - THE GREAT COMMISSION — 71
— Spiritual Keys
— Practical Keys
— Questions
— Reflection

7 WHAT'S NEXT? — 83
— Building Character
— Have Vision and Set Goals
— Questions
— Reflection

INTRODUCTION

The *Empowered IN HIM Study Guide* was written to equip, empower and activate you into all that God has called you to be.

We are all part of the body of Christ. Just as God created the different parts of our bodies to work together, He has also called us as the body of Christ to work together… each doing our part according to the gifts He has given. We have all been given different gifts, different spheres of influence, different parts, different anointings and grace for what He has called us to do.

When we say YES to Jesus, when we give Him our lives, we are signing up to be part of the army of God.

The Lord wants to use everyone in the Body of Christ to bring in the end-time harvest, and it is the responsibility of every believer to be teachable, to learn how to operate fully and effectively in the gifts of the Spirit.

The Bible says, *"Many are called but few are chosen"* (Matthew 22:14)
Why is it that some who profess to be Christians give their all for Jesus, holding nothing back, and others don't?

Salvation is a free gift.
The gifts of God are given freely.
The Father's love is given unconditionally.
But to actually be 'ALL IN' for God - to carry His anointing, to walk out His will and the calling He has for our lives, to stand against the enemy's plans, to move in the power of the Holy Spirit… costs us everything. It requires us to die to ourselves, lay down our own desires and refuse temptations.

The only limit to the power of God in YOUR life is YOU!

So many aren't willing to pay the price, to surrender all and completely rely on Him.

The gifts and callings of God are irrevocable,
but that does not mean that any person is irreplaceable."
Evangelist Daniel Kolenda

We all have a part to play in this season of the end-time harvest. What a remarkable time to be alive! I feel an urgency to encourage you to yield your life wholeheartedly to the call of God. Choosing to actively participate in God's amazing plans with the gifts He has given each of us is what is required in this season, because God and His plans will not be stopped.

Are YOU willing to pay the price?
Are YOU willing to truly live for Christ?
Are YOU willing to be part of the army of God?
Are YOU willing to make a stand?
Are YOU willing to step into all God has for you?

Every single one of us has been given gifts and talents by God to use for His glory. What God has gifted you with is not only for church meetings. To make an impact on earth for His Kingdom, we need to understand that His anointing is on us 24/7 – at home, at work, at school, on the sports fields, while shopping for groceries or wherever we find ourselves. These gifts are to be used NOW, they won't be of any use to us when we enter glory; no-one will need a prophetic word in heaven, no-one will need to be taught the Word, no-one will need saving!

Your gift is for NOW!

What are YOU doing with what He has given YOU?

HAVING THEN GIFTS......LET US USE THEM

(ROMANS 12:6)

1

INTIMACY
RELATIONSHIP WITH JESUS

Before we even think about anything else, we MUST start with relationship - intimacy with Jesus. Everything we do or say stems from this place. We were created to know Him!

Hunger, repentance, first love, secret place, prayer, abiding, worship, being filled, humility, holiness; these are some of the first words that come to mind when I think about intimacy and relationship with God.

There are a few key factors that come into play to be in a place of intimacy with the Lord, but it all starts with hunger! The bible says that, *"Those who hunger and thirst will be filled."* (Matthew 5:6). To receive an outpouring of His Spirit, we must be hungry!

When we hear of different places in the world where God shows up and remains, places thousands travel to from all over to meet with Him, where cities are shaken, where meetings go on for hours as the Spirit of God is poured out; this all happens because of hungry people who want God more than what's on TV that night, more than anything the world can offer, more than fame or fortune, and they're willing to lay aside everything to go after Him.

  HUNGRY PEOPLE ARE HUNGRY IN SECRET!

Too often we go from conference to conference, from altar call to altar call. We stand in

Empowered IN HIM Workbook

prayer lines wanting impartations from others who we see as anointed. However, they cannot impart to you their history with Jesus - the hours they have spent praying, the price they have paid, the things they have laid down - those things cannot be imparted. These things need to be built in us personally over time, as we hunger for more of God, as we continually lay down our lives, lay down our dreams and surrender to His will and His way for us.

Your level of hunger is indicative of how healthy you are in the Spirit. In the natural, when you are unwell, you lose your appetite (hunger is an indicator of health).

What are you feeding?

Every time you feed your flesh, you deaden your spiritual hunger. We must feed our spirit more than our flesh. How? We spend time in the Word, in prayer, in fellowship, and in worship. We spend time with Jesus. Time with Jesus is the MOST important thing.

It seems after we have been born again for a few years, we are not as hungry as we once were. We "mature", like the older brother in the story of the prodigal son; we calm down and become more reverent!

What actually happens is we lose our passion, we lose our first love, and we become apathetic and complacent. When we realise how far we've fallen, we get hungry, we start praying and cry out for revival and God pours His Spirit out again, satisfying our hunger.

The outpouring will only last as long as the hunger!

In Matthew 14 Jesus feeds the 5000, verse 20 says, *"And everyone ate until they were satisfied, for the food was multiplied in front of their eyes!"*
The bread stopped multiplying once they were satisfied. When you become content and satisfied with where you are, your hunger will fade. The outpouring will last as long as the hunger - there is always more!

It's so easy to become caught up in all the things the Lord does, forgetting who He is. We need to pursue the call to intimacy - sitting at His feet, staying in the secret place, abiding with Him. The secret place is where we build our relationship with Him. The secret place is where we hear His heart, where we learn to go deeper, where we encounter His love and beauty, where we learn to hear and obey His voice.

By remembering our 'burning bush', or our 'road to Damascus' experience, the defining moment when we encountered the Lord, will draw out our continual YES to Him. Stay in 'first love' with Him. Just as we keep the fire burning in our physical marriage by giving our husband or wife our full attention and our unwavering commitment, so too should we keep the first love fire burning for the Lord by relentlessly pursuing Him the way He pursues us. If we don't keep burning for Him, we will soon burn out.

Psalm 27:4 (AMP) says, *"One thing I have asked of the Lord, and that I will seek: That I may dwell in the house of the Lord [in His presence] all the days of my life, To gaze upon the beauty [the delightful loveliness and majestic grandeur] of the Lord, and to meditate in His temple."*

To gaze upon His beauty, to fix our eyes on Him alone … what beautiful imagery in this Psalm. Song of Songs, a beautiful book in the Bible, uses similar imagery. It is a love story of Christ and His bride (us). It talks about having dove's eyes - an undistracted focus on our Saviour.

The interesting thing about doves is that they have binocular vision, meaning that they can only focus on one thing at a time - usually it is their mate. When they look at their mate, they aren't distracted by anything else, their gaze is fixed on the one thing that matters. Doves have been nicknamed 'love birds'. If you watch a pair of doves, they are always watching each other, always doing what the other one does. Such an incredible picture of love and devotion and example for us to attain to.

Spending time with Jesus will have an effect on us that others will notice.

In Acts 4:13(TPT) it says, *"The council members were astonished as they witnessed the bold courage of Peter and John, especially when they discovered that they were just ordinary men who had never had religious training. Then they began to understand the effect Jesus had on them simply by spending time with him."*

Our first and highest calling is to minister to the Lord.

IF THE LORD'S SOLE PURPOSE FOR YOU IN THIS WORLD WAS TO MINISTER TO HIM ALONE, WOULD THAT BE ENOUGH FOR YOU?

The Bible says to, *"Love the Lord your God which ALL your heart, ALL your mind, ALL your strength..."* everything else is an overflow of this. We can't give to others what we don't have ourselves. We can't lead others somewhere we haven't been. We can't teach others something we haven't learnt.

Questions

How often and how much time do you spend in the word?

_____
_____
_____
_____
_____
_____
_____
_____

How often and how much time do you spend in prayer?

_____
_____
_____
_____
_____
_____
_____

How often and how much time do you spend in worship?

_____
_____
_____
_____
_____
_____
_____

How can you improve on the amount and the quality of time you spend in the Word? In prayer? In worship? Think of your daily habits or schedules; how could you adapt them to make time for these things?

_____
_____
_____
_____
_____
_____
_____
_____
_____
_____
_____
_____
_____
_____
_____
_____
_____
_____
_____
_____
_____
_____
_____
_____

What are 3 other things you can do to build and deepen your relationship with the Lord?

Reflection

Ask the Lord, "What is your favourite way to spend time with me?"
What's the first thing that pops into your head? Write or draw what He shows you.

Reflection

Reflection

2
OUR IDENTITY

We must be solid in our identity. Before Jesus ever worked one miracle or spoke one parable, He was loved and accepted by God. After Jesus was baptised, in Matthew 3:17, it says, *"And a voice from heaven said, "This is My beloved Son, in whom I am well pleased!""*

In the same way, we are already loved by the Father, He is already pleased with us. We don't have to earn His love and acceptance. Romans 5:8 (AMP) says, *"But God clearly shows and proves His own love for us, by the fact that while we were still sinners, Christ died for us."*

*THERE IS NOTHING WE CAN DO TO MAKE GOD LOVE US ANY MORE **OR** ANY LESS!*

Knowing who we are and Whose we are - knowing that we are beloved children of the King - forgiven, accepted, favoured, made righteous, victorious, chosen, redeemed, blessed, treasured, healed, justified, an overcomer, free, more than a conqueror ... the list goes on. Search out these promises in the word and speak them over yourself.

Knowing what we have - we have been given every spiritual blessing, we have been given the armour of God, we have the assurance of heaven, we have peace with God, we have access to grace, we have the Holy Spirit!

Knowing where we are seated - in Heavenly places, together with Christ, far above all principalities and powers.

Empowered IN HIM Workbook

Knowing what we can do - ALL THINGS, through HIM!

We don't need to try to be children of God, the word of God says we already are! Just like my children don't need to strive and try to be my kids - they just are!

One of the most important revelations we can get from the Word of God is to understand who we are in Christ. Identifying with Christ will change the way we live, not understanding our identity in Him will keep us living far below our rights and privileges in Christ.

Unfortunately, some Christians are having an identity crisis. They don't know who they are in Christ or where they are seated. Instead of identifying with Christ, they identify with the problems that confront them. You can tell they do this because they call themselves by their problems: divorced, bankrupt, and so forth.
Some identify with a profession and say things like, "I'm a salesman," or "I'm a lawyer." But their profession is not who they are; it's what they do. Others identify with the disease that is attacking their bodies. They say, "I'm a diabetic," "I'm ADD," or "I am bipolar."
When we really understand our identity in Christ—who we are in Him—it changes the way we think and live.

What God says about us is found in His Word. Here are some things we are and have in Christ:
We are children of God (1 John 3:1)
We are a chosen people (Col. 3:12)
We are loved (Romans 5:8)
We are forgiven (1 John 1:9)
We are seated in Heavenly places (Eph 2:6)
We are new creatures (2 Cor. 5:17)
We are the righteousness of God (2 Cor. 5:21)
We've been healed (1 Peter 2:24)
We've been made rich (2 Cor. 8:9)
We are accepted (Eph. 1:6)
We are free from sin (Rom. 6:20–22)

Instead of **SINNER**, you are called **SON or DAUGHTER**
Instead of **LOST**, you are called **FOUND**.
Instead of **ENEMY**, you are called **FRIEND**.
Instead of **UNRIGHTEOUS**, you are called **RIGHTEOUS**.
Instead of **SICK**, you are called **HEALED**.
Instead of **POOR**, you are called **RICH**.

When you understand your identity in Christ, you'll be stronger, your prayer life will be richer, and you'll walk in a new level of authority.

Using the picture of an iceberg as an example; the top of the iceberg is you - your ministry, your gifts or what people see. Below is what you have built on - the time you have spent with God, your identity, your character, your integrity.

INTIMACY

IDENTITY

INTEGRITY

INFLUENCE

IMPACT

Empowered IN HIM Workbook

Search out the scriptures, find your identity IN HIM!

We cannot base our identity on WHAT WE DO, but on WHO WE ARE! We are loved and accepted by the King of kings regardless of what we do for Him.

It should never be about performance, identity, acceptance (in that order), but rather acceptance, identity, performance. What we do comes from the overflow of who we are! When we are confident in our identity, we won't be trying to please people, but whatever we do, it will be unto the Lord.

Finally, the fruit (or results) of this intimacy with God (after we have allowed Him to change us and we have become confident in our identity IN HIM) will affect the world around us - our families, our communities, our towns and cities, our regions, our state and our nations.
Being filled with God is not just for us. We need to let Him overflow out of us. The Bible talks about *"rivers of living water"* flowing out from us, (John 7:38).

Questions

Do you know who you are IN HIM?

Are you confident in your identity?

Are you striving to please God or living from the overflow of who you are IN HIM?

What adjustments do you need to make?

Reflection

Take a few deep breaths, quieten your heart and ask your heavenly Father to show you what He thinks when He looks at you. What is the expression on His face? Then ask Him what it is that He loves about you. Write or draw what He shows you.

Reflection

Reflection

3
BALANCING MINISTRY AND FAMILY

Second only to God is our family. Our order of priorities should always be God first, then family, then ministry.

In 1 Timothy chapter 3 the Bible speaks of the qualifications of those in leadership, and in verse 5 it says, *"For if a man cannot manage his own household, how can he take care of God's church?"*
Loving our family, making sure we are intentional about our time with them, making sure we are fully present in that time, making sure we are reading the Bible and praying together, must come before any commitments we make to church or ministry or work.

Too many people who have stepped out in ministry have sacrificed their families whilst pursuing what they felt God has called them to. However, our very first ministry after the Lord, must be to our families. If our family is seeing us behave differently at home compared to what everyone else is seeing, we are doing something wrong.

Our spouse and our children deserve our best, not our leftovers. Family dinners and date nights are important!! Set aside time just for each other regularly, with NO DISTRACTIONS! Turn off your phones! Create boundaries!

The Bible says to *"train up a child in the way he should go"*, (Proverbs 22:6) This is a Biblical promise parents! In Ephesians 6:4 it says to *"bring them up in the training and instruction of the Lord."*

Empowered IN HIM Workbook

Our children are a gift (Psalm 127:3), not a burden. If God has entrusted us with children, it is our responsibility (not the Sunday school teacher's), to ensure they are bought up to know Him in the way He has directed us to.

How tragic would it be to save the world but lose your children.

Daily devotions and prayer time together is a MUST! Whether you have children or not, it is important to spend time in the Word and in prayer together as a couple or as a family.

Our families need to know that apart from God they are our first priority; before church, before work, before ministry. No matter how passionate we are about the call to ministry on our lives, our families need to know that they are MORE important.

Enter into what God has for you together as a family. Don't let your children miss out on the joy of serving. Involve them, encourage them to step out themselves, celebrate with them.

As well as serving the Lord and ministering together, it's equally important to have fun together ensure that when you do have time off, you are having fun!

For some, there may not be natural family around, but as Christians we are also part of a much bigger family - Kingdom family. Just like natural families, it is important to do life with each other, to be intentional about our time together, being present in those moments and praying together.

Man was never made to be alone. We all need fellowship, community and support, however, because we are all human and live in a fallen world, we may not always agree with one another. But this can be a good thing, as Proverbs 27:17 says, *"As irons sharpens iron, so one person sharpens another."*
On the journey of doing life together, there are good times and bad times, but the Bible warns us against things like gossip, jealousy and division, but instead teaches us to live with gentleness, humility, perseverance and kindness.

In fact, the Word says to love one another, forgive one another, honour one another, and by this the world will know that we are His disciples. It says when we live together in unity, He will command a blessing.

Once we have these foundational things in place with those around us, in our immediate world, it is so much easier to live all-in for God. Our families (both natural and spiritual) will be ready for whatever God calls us to do, because we're already living the way we should both at home and at church; so we can work together to bring the right balance.

We know that to live "all in" means sacrifice and selflessness, spontaneity and flexibility, it means serving and work, and dying to self. But we also know our bodies need to rest and our families need our attention, so we need to make time to relax, for date nights, beach days, family fun, holidays, etc.

We must learn to steward whatever it is that the Lord wants to pour out. To do this well, we need to balance our time, to use it wisely and to make space for different seasons whilst remaining flexible to the wind of the Spirit. This, again, brings us back to *abiding IN HIM*.

Questions

Is your family getting your best or what is left?

_____
_____
_____
_____
_____
_____
_____

Is your family seeing the same person at home as they see outside of the home?

_____
_____
_____
_____
_____
_____
_____

In what ways can you improve your family devotion time?

_____
_____
_____
_____
_____
_____
_____

What are some ways you can have fun together?

_____
_____
_____
_____
_____
_____
_____
_____
_____
_____
_____
_____
_____
_____
_____

How can you involve your family in serving/ministry?

_____
_____
_____
_____
_____
_____
_____
_____

Reflection

Ask your family those same questions.

4
THE FIVE-FOLD GIFTS

The five-fold ministry and gifts of the Spirit are vital subjects to know and fully understand. Five-fold is a term we use to refer to the gifts of the Spirit as referred to in Ephesians 4:11.

It is so important to have a Biblical understanding so that we, as the body of Christ, can function according to God's will and His plan.

It is imperative that we know our gifts, our callings and our commission so that we can minister to the right people, at the right place, at the right time, under the right anointing. Trying to make a pastor or teacher out of someone whom God has called to be an evangelist, will never work because that is not the calling or gift on their life. We can still MOVE in different spiritual gifts, like, for example, an evangelist could also move powerfully in the gift of prophecy. It's all about knowing what your mandate is and learning how to walk in it.

Imagine the transformation in our homes, workplaces or schools, or wherever we find ourselves, when we realise the power available to us to reveal God's love for people as we use the gifts God has given us. You can walk in the gift God has given you, whether as a prophet, teacher, evangelist, pastor or apostle, or any of the spiritual gifts mentioned in 1 Corinthians chapter 12, wherever you are.

Over the following pages, we will take a little more of an in-depth look at each of the five-fold ministry gifts, which are Apostle, Prophet, Teacher, Pastor and Evangelist,

Empowered IN HIM Workbook

along with their roles in the church and the characteristics of these gifts.

It is also necessary to understand the difference between the office of a particular gift and the gift itself, i.e. the 'office of a prophet' or the 'gift of prophecy'. The office of a prophet is a full time calling and refers specifically to a person's calling or leadership role within the church, while the gift of prophecy is a spiritual gift available to all believers.

The gifts of the Spirit are for everyone who has been born again and filled with the Holy Spirit. We are encouraged in 1 Corinthians chapter 14 to, *"earnestly desire the spiritual gifts"*.

In this section we will be focusing specifically on the five-fold gifts and the following section on the gifts of the Spirit we read about in 1 Corinthians chapter 12.

The 'offices' are not man-made, nor can they be taught in a school or training session. These are gifts with anointing given by Christ Himself to those whom He chooses.

Ephesians 4:11-13 (NKJV) says, *"And He Himself gave some to be apostles, some prophets, some evangelists, and some pastors and teachers, for the equipping of the saints for the work of ministry, for the edifying of the body of Christ, till we all come to the unity of the faith and of the knowledge of the Son of God, to a perfect man, to the measure of the stature of the fullness of Christ;"*

Jesus Himself functioned in all of the five-fold ministry gifts while He was on earth and is the perfect role model for us. One thing we see in Christ's example is that we need the anointing of the Holy Spirit. It was not until Jesus was baptised and the Holy Spirit came upon Him that He started His earthly ministry; before that He hadn't healed one person or done one miracle! So, just like Jesus, we need the anointing of the Holy Spirit to operate in the five-fold offices.

EARNESTLY DESIRE THE SPIRITUAL GIFTS
(1 CORINTHIANS 14:1)

A call to the five-fold ministry is firstly affirmed by God to the individual, then at a later stage, the gift or calling would be recognised and be affirmed by people, generally by other members of the five-fold ministry.

Those who are called into the five-fold ministry must also realise they will be held to higher standards - greater accountability and judgement - it is definitely not something to be taken lightly. (Hebrews 13:17, James 3:1, 1 Peter 5:2-3, Titus 1:6-9).

Each of the five-fold ministries do not work in isolation, their functions are intricately interwoven as their gifts overlap, intermingle and complement each other. They are woven together by the seamless thread of God. I recently heard this illustration of the five-fold ministries working together:
"*Apostles set the course, prophets direct people to get on the course, evangelists gather and lead people to run the course, pastors guard and maintain people in the right course, while teachers instruct and groom people to mature on the course.*"

We must remember that we are called to SERVE. A calling into the ministry isn't about a position or a platform, it is a call to serve the body - to direct, to nurture, to protect, to love, to correct, to teach, to lead, and to prepare the Bride for the return of her Bridegroom.

WHAT ARE THE FIVE OFFICES OF THE FIVE-FOLD MINISTRY?
The hand is a simple analogy to help illustrate the five-fold ministry.

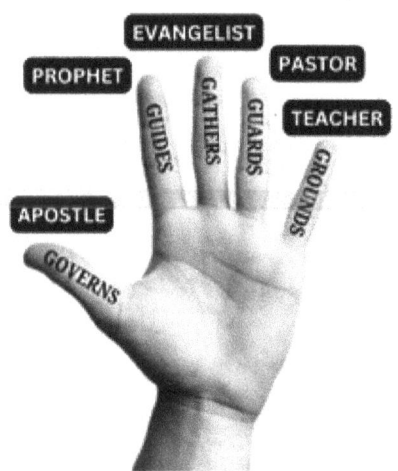

Empowered IN HIM Workbook

1. The thumb is the Apostle. This office is represented by the thumb, as the thumb can easily touch each of the other fingers on a person's hand, meaning the apostle can function in all five gifts.

2. The pointer finger is the Prophet. The prophet gives direction and guidance.

3. The middle finger is the Evangelist because they have the most reach. The evangelist's role is to gather and spread the gospel.

4. The ring finger is the Pastor, representing their marriage to the sheep. The pastor's role is to guard the sheep, to nurture and care for the flock.

5. The pinkie finger is the Teacher because they bring balance to the body of Christ with the grounding in the word.

Only when each of these ministries have come into complete unity, will they attain to the fullness of their own individual callings and then be able to perfect the Bride in readiness for the Bridegroom.

If we feel called to the specific five-fold ministry, we should seek to find a mentor that we can submit ourselves to who is already walking in the relevant office and allow them to speak into our lives, be accountable to them, serve them, learn from them. Never graduate from having a spiritual covering.

Before you move on to have a look at the characteristics of each of the five-fold gifts, first work through some questions and reflections.

Questions

Which of the five-fold gifts (if any), do you feel most called to?

_____
_____
_____
_____
_____
_____
_____

If you feel called to a certain five-fold gift, does this mean you will hold the "office" of that gift?

_____
_____
_____
_____
_____
_____
_____

What are the five-fold ministry gifts for?

_____
_____
_____
_____
_____
_____
_____

Reflection

Ask the Father how you can use your gift(s) to serve your local church. Then ask Him to show you how you can use your gift(s) to serve your family. Then ask him how you can use your gift(s) to serve the people at your workplace (if you have one).

Reflection

Reflection

APOSTLE
The Apostle Governs

Jesus stood in the office of an apostle - Hebrew 3:1 says, *"Therefore, holy brethren, partakers of the heavenly calling, consider the Apostle and High Priest of our confession, Christ Jesus."*

The meaning of the word apostle is SENT ONE, one sent with authority on a mission. The apostle is the dream awakener, the trailblazer, the pioneer, the trend setter, the record breaker.

The calling of an apostle is a call to lead leaders. An apostle thinks big, bigger than one place or one group of people. They have a desire to train and raise up leaders, then release them.

They are visionary and their vision pushes them to take new spiritual ground beyond what currently exists in the local church. An apostle is an entrepreneur with a strong desire to pioneer.

An apostle has a strong ability to influence and lead, they have a great capacity to draw others into the work of God.

They are grounded in the word and have a burden to ground the church in solid biblical teaching. (Acts 11 - Paul and Barnabas spent two years teaching and equipping).

"While evangelists create converts, apostles create disciples." Kim Terrell

Apostles move in the supernatural. This office flows in and out of each of the five-fold offices as needed. The apostle brings establishment, order and leadership to the five-fold ministries.

Are you apostolic? Do these characteristics describe you personally? If God has given you this gift, He has a way for you to use it to build His church.

Here are a few ideas to steward the apostolic gift:
- Plant and submit yourself in a church under an apostolic leader, a kingdom church that is passionate about recognising the call of God, raising up and releasing people into their destiny
- Look for new ways to pioneer the gospel, investing your efforts where they will be put to use
- Walk in humility
- Rest in your identity as a son or daughter of the King
- Remember your first ministry is to the Lord

REFLECTION

REFLECTION

PROPHET
The Prophet Guides

Jesus stood in the office of a prophet; in fact, He called Himself a prophet. In Luke 4:24 it says, *"Then He said, 'Assuredly, I say to you, no prophet is accepted in his own country.'"*

Scripture tells us that we can all hear God's Voice, *"My sheep know My voice."* (John 10:27) and we can all prophesy (1 Corinthians 14:31), it's a gift to each member of the body to be used for edification and exhortation, however, operating in the gift of prophecy and being called into the office of a prophet is very different. The prophetic anointing is an impartation of God's supernatural ability upon a chosen person in order for them to speak the mind of God and reveal His heart.

A prophet's role is not to prophesy over individuals (although they have the gift to do that), their role is to teach the church how to hear God for themselves.

A prophet points the way. They are called to direct, warn, correct, train and guide the church. A prophet reveals Gods heart and mind to His people.

The prophet is a watchman, a trumpet-blower, keeping an eye on what is happening and giving direction.

A prophet is a seer, who sees things others cannot see and is the messenger of these things to the church. They would have dreams and visions, they would operate in the gifts of words of wisdom and words of knowledge.

It is imperative that the prophet develops a sensitivity to move in the Spirit realm. Prophetic training, consecration, renewing of the mind and removing distractions will make it easier to flow in the prophetic gift.

Examples of prophets in the Bible are: Silas (Acts 15:32), Isaiah, Jeremiah, Daniel, Hosea, Jeremiah, Samuel, Micah, Jonah...to name just a few.

REFLECTION

PASTOR
The Pastor Guards

Jesus stood in the office of a pastor. He testified saying, *"I am the Good Shepherd"* (John 10:14), and Peter called Jesus the *"Chief Shepherd"* in 1 Peter 5:4.

The office of a pastor is probably the most recognised of the five-fold ministry, mainly because of the lack of understanding of the other four gifts.

The word pastor appears only once in the New Testament and translated as 'shepherd'.

A pastor is a shepherd. He cares deeply for the sheep and his greatest concern is the well-being of those he has been entrusted with.

His desire is that his flock are fed, nurtured and protected, that they grow and mature, and that they are equipped and trained in their individual gifting.
A pastor would have a strong giftings of teaching, healing and administration. His ministry duties would include visitations, counselling, conducting weddings and funerals, prayer gatherings as well as the overseeing the local church.

Those who have the five-fold gifting of prophet, evangelist, teachers and apostle are often placed in the position of pastor, but do not have the patience or the grace to care for and feed the sheep.

The pastor creates an atmosphere of family and belonging. They are concerned for people's hearts and emotions, they embrace people and make them feel included. They protect but also bring training and correction.

In order for the church to operate effectively, the person walking in the five-fold gift of a pastor must realise they need the other four gifts. The pastor is the bridge between the church and the other ministries of the five-fold.

REFLECTION

EVANGELIST
The Evangelist Gathers

Jesus stood in the office of an evangelist. He said in Luke 4:18, *"The Spirit of the Lord is upon me, because He has anointed me to preach the gospel to the poor."*

The office of an evangelist is a unique calling and their place in the five-fold ministry is absolutely crucial to the growth of the local church and the kingdom of God.

One of the roles of the evangelist is to keep the whole body (not just other evangelists) focused on preaching the Gospel and winning the lost. While an evangelist's passion is to see souls come into the kingdom, they are not primarily soul winners but are also called to stir up the church and move its people into action.

Evangelists love teaching others how to win people to Christ and are grieved when they see the complacency and indifference from the believers towards those who don't know Him.

The evangelist is anointed to preach the Gospel with the demonstration of signs, wonders and miracles often following. They can flow in both the prophetic gift and also in healing. When proclaiming the Gospel, the evangelist will preach for the salvation of souls.

"The evangelist proclaims, while the teacher explains." Unknown

The evangelist anointing is one of the most powerful anointings given by God because the main business of the church is winnings souls.
The Webster dictionary defines evangelism as the act of winning, or revival, of personal commitments to Christ.
The Bible mentions the word evangelist three times: Phillip the evangelist (Acts 21), the gift of an evangelist (Ephesians 4) and the work of an evangelist (2 Timothy).

The 'gift' of an evangelist and the 'work' of an evangelist are two different things. In the Bible, Paul tells Timothy to do the work of an evangelist even though that was not his gift. We are ALL called to evangelise (or be a witness), it is simply an overflow of what is on the inside of us.

When you are in love with someone, you can't help but talk about them. It is the same with Christ; when we encounter His love, we can't help but tell others about Him.

An evangelist, while needed in the church, will also be itinerant, his reach will go further than the local church and community. An evangelist in today's church would generally oversee outreach and mission teams, train and equip others in the same gifting, maintain passion and vision within the church for the lost and winning souls.

Examples: Peter, Stephen, the Woman at the Well and Phillip.

REFLECTION

_____
_____
_____
_____
_____
_____
_____
_____
_____
_____
_____
_____
_____
_____
_____
_____
_____

REFLECTION

TEACHER
The Teacher Grounds

Jesus stood in the office of a teacher; it was His priority. He taught more than He preached, He taught more than He healed. The Bible says in John 3:2, *"This man came to Jesus and said to Him, 'Rabbi, we know that you are a teacher come from God: for no-one can do these signs that You do unless God is with him.'"*

It takes all of the five-fold ministries to perfect the church and a very important gift of bringing Christian believers to maturity is the Bible teacher.

All believers can, and are encouraged, to share Scripture with others. Some can do it quite effectively. But just as winning a soul doesn't make a person an Ephesians 4:11 evangelist, likewise, being able to teach reasonably well doesn't make one an Ephesians 4:11 teacher.

The teacher may be led into deeper study of certain specialties, for example, end times, New Testament, or Old Testament, etc. But every teacher should have a working knowledge of the entirety of the word.

The teacher has an insatiable love for God's word. He has a broad and deep knowledge of the Word. He spends much time studying the Bible, learning, developing and cultivating his gift. He speaks with authority and is clearly gifted by the Holy Spirit for this ministry. He has the patience to teach systematically, verse-by-verse, as well as topically, year after year.

The teacher, like the other five-fold ministry gifts, is motivated to see believers perfected. Their desire is to dissect the Word of God to make sure the church thoroughly understands the truth of scripture.

James chapter 3 has a specific warning for those who are teaching: the office of a teacher is not something to be taken lightly. James 3:1 (NLT) says, *"Not many of you should become teachers, my fellow believers, because you know that we who teach will be judged more strictly."*

If we ourselves believe bad doctrine, it will be a negative influence in our own life. But if we teach bad doctrine, we spread the corrupting influence beyond ourselves to others.

Teaching cannot be purely academic: a teacher's life will line up with what he teachers. He must be diligent to maintain a close walk with the Lord, and that will be evident in what he is teaching.

If you have the gift of teaching then you need to develop and cultivate that gift; study, prepare, and broaden your knowledge in the word. Devote time to worshiping the Lord and developing your own spiritual life so that you aren't just teaching the word but being a living example of it.

REFLECTION

_____
_____
_____
_____
_____
_____
_____
_____
_____
_____
_____
_____
_____
_____
_____
_____
_____

REFLECTION

5
ADDITIONAL SPIRITUAL GIFTS

Along with the five-fold gifts, there are many other gifts mentioned in the word that are equally important for the body of Christ to function properly.

Some may have the gift of hospitality and service that is mentioned in
1 Peter 4:9-11 (AMP), *"Just as each one of you has received a special gift [a spiritual talent, an ability graciously given by God], employ it in serving one another as [is appropriate for] good stewards of God's multi-faceted grace [faithfully using the diverse, varied gifts and abilities granted to Christians by God's unmerited favour]. Whoever speaks [to the congregation], is to do so as one who speaks the oracles (utterances, the very words) of God. Whoever serves [the congregation] is to do so as one who serves by the strength which God [abundantly] supplies, so that in all things God may be glorified [honoured and magnified] through Jesus Christ, to whom belongs the glory and dominion forever and ever. Amen."*

We can also be gifted in worship, administration, encouragement/exhortation, mercy, business or marketplace ministry and many, many more areas. ALL are needed!

Just as a human body needs all the parts working together to function, so to for the body of Christ to be fully effective, each one of us needs to be operating in the gifts He has called us to.

In 1 Corinthians chapter 12, Paul states the nine gifts of the Spirit are given (by the Holy Spirit), for the edification of the church.

Empowered IN HIM Workbook

These are:

1. Word of Wisdom
2. Word of Knowledge
3. Gift of Faith
4. Gift of Healing
5. Miracles
6. Gift of Prophecy
7. Gift of Discernment
8. Speaking in Tongues
9. Interpretation of Tongues

In Romans chapter 12 Paul says, *"For just as in one [physical] body we have many parts, and these parts do not all have the same function or special use, so we, who are many, are [nevertheless just] one body in Christ, and individually [we are] parts one of another [mutually dependent on each other]. Since we have gifts that differ according to the grace given to us, each of us is to use them accordingly: if [someone has the gift of] prophecy, [let him speak a new message from God to His people] in proportion to the faith possessed; if service, in the act of serving; or he who teaches, in the act of teaching; or he who encourages, in the act of encouragement; he who gives, with generosity; he who leads, with diligence; he who shows mercy [in caring for others], with cheerfulness."* (Romans 12:4-8 AMP)

For each gift, there is a unique grace for that ministry, as above in Romans 12:6, *"we have gifts that differ according to the grace given to us"*. If we try to operate outside of that grace, we will fail not only ourselves but those we are ministering to.

HOW DO I KNOW WHAT MY SPIRITUAL GIFT/S ARE?
There are different ways to find the answer to this question, but firstly - pray! Ask the Lord, He is the One who created you and He knows the plans He has for you.

REFLECTION

Stay in the Word, study the different gifts and pay attention to what you are drawn to. Be sensitive to the leading of the Holy Spirit.

Your gifts will determine your response to certain circumstance or situations. For example, you are told by a friend that their mother is in hospital with a very serious illness.

If you have the **gift of healing**, you will want to go straight to the hospital to anoint, pray and believe for your friend's mother to be healed.

If you have the **gift of service (or helps)**, you will ask in what practical ways you can help by for e.g. cook meals, look after your friend's children or pets so they can do hospital visits, do errands to help lessen the burden, etc.

If you have the **gift of encouragement**, you will aim to brighten the situation. Bring flowers, give hugs, encourage laughter, all with the express purpose of improving their frame of mind.

One important point to remember:

THE GIFTS OF THE HOLY SPIRIT
WITHOUT THE FRUIT OF THE HOLY SPIRIT
WILL NEVER WORK.

In order to operate in the gifts, we must first display the fruit. (See chapter 7-Building Character)

"But the fruit of the Spirit is love, joy, peace, longsuffering, kindness, goodness, faithfulness, gentleness, self-control. Against such there is no law. And those who are Christ's have crucified the flesh with its passions and desires. If we live in the Spirit, let us also walk in the Spirit." (Galatians 5:22-25)

THE GIFTS OF THE HOLY SPIRT WITHOUT THE FRUIT OF THE HOLY SPIRIT WILL NEVER WORK

Questions

What are your strongest gifts?

_____
_____
_____
_____
_____
_____
_____

In what area of ministry do you feel called?

_____
_____
_____
_____
_____
_____
_____
_____
_____
_____
_____
_____
_____
_____
_____

What are your frustrations within the church (this can often be a sign of what area you are called to)?

What area of serving/ministry gives you the greatest satisfaction?

What are some things you can do to develop the areas you feel God has called you to?

_____
_____
_____
_____
_____
_____
_____
_____
_____
_____
_____
_____
_____
_____
_____
_____
_____
_____
_____
_____
_____
_____
_____
_____
_____
_____
_____

Reflection

Ask Jesus, "Lord, which of the fruits of your Spirit would you like to grow in me in the next month?"

Reflection

Reflection

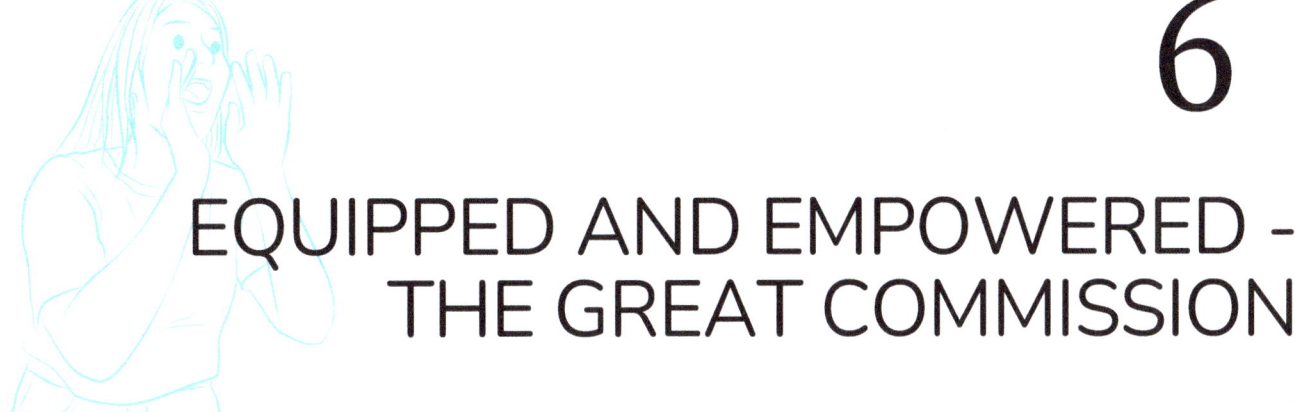

6
EQUIPPED AND EMPOWERED - THE GREAT COMMISSION

Regardless of your individual gift or calling, we are all called to fulfil the great commission. God is calling His church to step out of mediocrity and into the fullness of what He has destined for her.

Acts 1:8 says, *"But you shall receive power when the Holy Spirit has come upon you; and **you shall be witnesses** to Me in Jerusalem, and in all Judea and Samaria, and to the end of the earth."* (emphasis added)

Above all, when we are saved and receive the Holy Spirit we are called to be witnesses. So, regardless of our gifts, callings, talents and abilities, we are all empowered by the Holy Spirit to preach the gospel!

WHY?

Because Jesus commanded it. Time is short and the harvest is ripe - the only thing we can take with us when we leave this world is people!!

And He said to them, *"Go into all the world and preach the gospel to every creature."* (Mark 16:15)

The great commission is not an 'optional extra' for a Christian, it is what we are called to do, and it all begins with being a witness for Him. We are ALL called to be witnesses. As a follower of Christ, we are all called to share the Gospel, and why would we not?? If we truly believe what we say we believe, wouldn't we want everyone to know about Jesus - we alone have the hope of all humanity!

"The Great Commission is not an option to be considered; it is a command to be obeyed."
Hudson Taylor

Empowered IN HIM Workbook

YOU SHALL BE WITNESSES TO ME
(ACTS 1:8)

In Acts, the early church evangelized EVERY DAY...after just being flogged for doing so. Acts 5:42 (AMP) says, *"And every single day, in the temple [area] and in homes, they did not stop teaching and telling the good news of Jesus as the Christ (the Messiah, the Anointed)."*

HOW?
There are so many different ways to share the Gospel, so many different places and spheres in society we can evangelize, so many different people to reach. We are all different and you are going to reach people that others cannot.

Street evangelism, open air preaching, one to one, homeless outreach and programs, event outreach, missions, prison ministry, workplace and many, many more are all ways we can share Christ. We can do something as simple as making a meal for a neighbour who is sick, or we can preach to thousands at a crusade in Africa - all are necessary and effective ways to reach the lost.

"The simple definition of evangelism: Those who know, telling those who don't." Leith Anderson

Evangelism doesn't need to be difficult; your testimony is a perfect place to start. A personal testimony is a description of what has happened in your life as a result of an encounter with Jesus. Every follower of Christ has a story of what God has done for them. Sometimes we only have a very short time to sow a seed, sometimes we have longer. It's a great idea to have your testimony ready for all opportunities.

A thirty second version could be something like this, "I was a drug addict, a dealer, caught up in all sorts of crime and one day, on the way to get drugs, I ran out of petrol right outside a minister's house. Instead of getting drugs that day, I met God when I wasn't even looking for Him and He changed my life forever. He showed me love, He took me at my lowest and loved me right there in my mess. He set me free from a lifestyle of drugs and crime.

Empowered IN HIM Workbook

He has given me a life full of peace and joy...He can do the same for you!"
(This is my personal thirty second version!) Have a five minute version and a thirty minute version ready also, for longer conversations.

Revelation 12:11, *"And they overcame him (the enemy) by the blood of the Lamb, and by the word of their testimony..."*
Your testimony is a powerful tool, it demonstrates the reality of the Gospel. It impacts the person listening and reminds you of where you have come from and what God has done for you.

WHEN?
ALL THE TIME!! Evangelism is not just for events or outreach. Evangelism is a lifestyle. The Bible says to, *"...preach the word [as an official messenger]; be ready when the time is right and even when it is not [keep your sense of urgency, whether the opportunity seems favourable or unfavourable, whether convenient or inconvenient, whether welcome or unwelcome]; correct [those who err in doctrine or behaviour], warn [those who sin], exhort and encourage [those who are growing toward spiritual maturity, with inexhaustible patience and [faithful] teaching."* (2 Timothy 4:2, AMP)

Statistics show that 96% of Christians in the Western world do not share their faith. This needs to change. Let's start right here!!

"At the end of the day, the biggest obstacle to evangelism is Christians who don't share the gospel." Albert Mohler

We should ALWAYS be ready to share our faith: 1 Peter 3:15 (NLT) says, *"And if someone asks about your hope as a believer, always be ready to explain it."*

Spiritual Keys
- PRAY FIRST-You can't give what you haven't got!
- Spend time with Jesus, get to know Him intimately. Know His heart, know His voice. Pray for opportunities. Be led by the Holy Spirit. Pray for divine appointments.

- Pray for those who are lost, you are going to minister to people - they are NOT projects or numbers. Before you speak to a man about God, first speak to God about man!

"Prayer is crucial in evangelism: Only God can change the heart of someone who is in rebellion against Him. No matter how logical our arguments or how fervent our appeals, our words will accomplish nothing unless God's Spirit prepares the way." Billy Graham

Pray for salvations and healings and expect God to move, expect people to be saved and healed. When we preach the Gospel - the Gospel happens.

"For I am not ashamed of the gospel, for it is the power of God for salvation [from His wrath and punishment] to everyone who believes..."
(Romans 1:16, AMP)

The Bible says that His word will not return void.
"For just as rain and snow fall from heaven and do not return without watering the earth, making it bud and sprout, and providing seed to sow and food to eat, so My word that proceeds from My mouth will not return to Me empty, but it will accomplish what I please, and it will prosper where I send it." (Isaiah 55:10-11, BSB)

ABC's of the Gospel
Avoid debating theology or doctrines, stick to the basics of the Gospel: creation > fall > redemption > restoration.

1. GOD LOVES YOU AND HAS A PLAN FOR YOU.

2. SIN SEPARATES US FROM GOD, BUT NOT GOD'S LOVE FOR US.

3. JESUS CHRIST'S LIFE, DEATH, AND RESURRECTION REDEEMED US FROM SIN AND RESTORES GODS PLAN, ALLOWING US TO BECOME ADOPTED SONS and DAUGHTERS OF GOD.

4. TURN AWAY FROM SIN, TURN TO JESUS CHRIST, AND JOIN GOD'S FAMILY BY RECEIVING HIS FREE GIFT OF SALVATION

"Before I can call upon Christ as my Saviour, I have to understand that I need a saviour. I have to understand that I am a sinner. I have to have some understanding of what sin is. I have to understand that God exists. I have to understand that I am estranged from that God, and that I am exposed to that God's judgment. I don't reach out for a saviour unless I am first convinced that I need a saviour. All of that is pre-evangelism. It is involved in the data or the information that a person has to process with his mind before he can either respond to it in faith or reject it in unbelief. The Gospel is only good news when we understand the bad news." R. C. Sproul

Practical Keys
- Good hygiene - deodorant, breath mints. There is nothing worse than bad breath or bad body odour.
- Appropriate dress - please dress modestly. Dressing in revealing clothes is distracting.
- Smile - you are giving the GOOD news. Smile and be friendly.
- DON'T BE WEIRD - (This one is from our friend Daz Chettle). Do not use 'christianese' - language that a non-believer wouldn't understand. Use wisdom when speaking in tongues out loud with unbelievers or new believers, and explain what it is if you do.
- Don't argue - there is no point in arguing; if someone doesn't agree or doesn't want to listen, just let them know that God loves them. Avoid theology or doctrines. Stick to the ABC'S of the Gospel and use your testimony.
- Don't pretend you know everything. It's okay to say, 'I don't know'.
- Listen - we all have two ears and one mouth. Ask questions, listen and be responsive when people talk.
- BE YOU don't try to be someone else, be who God called you to be. You will connect with some people when others cannot.

Empowered IN HIM Workbook

- Praying: when praying for someone, always ask first. Always ask if the person is comfortable if you lay your hands on them when praying, and only ever lay a gentle hand on their shoulder or hold their hand.
- Respect personal space - we've all heard of social distancing, lol! Don't encroach on a person's personal space.
- Don't try to fit in – we are called to be the LIGHT of the world; we should look different. Don't smoke, don't do drugs or alcohol and don't swear just to fit in.

The assignment of the great commission though, is much more than evangelizing; that is only the beginning of the task. New converts must also be discipled, taught, nurtured, equipped, empowered and then sent out, which is why we need the whole body working together, each walking in their gifting and doing their part.

To walk out this journey of life the way God intended us to do, we need to become Empowered IN HIM! Equipped, activated and EMPOWERED by the Holy Spirit.

Questions

Regardless of our gifts, what are we ALL called to do?

_____
_____
_____
_____

What are some ways that I can be a witness to those in my sphere of influence?

_____
_____
_____
_____
_____
_____
_____
_____
_____
_____
_____
_____
_____
_____
_____
_____
_____

Write out your thirty second testimony.

Reflection

Ask the Lord to show you someone He would like you to share your 30 second testimony with. Ask Him to give you an opportunity to do so.

Reflection

Reflection

7
WHAT'S NEXT?

Building Character

To be able to walk in and SUSTAIN the gift and calling that God has on our life, we need to develop our character. I have heard it said often, "Character cradles the Call" or "Character before Anointing", and it is so true!

Without our character being built first, we will be unable to fully walk in and sustain all that God has called us to. It's easy to start off excitement and determination, but when the tests and trials come (and they will definitely come), we need the endurance to be able to stay the course.

If we want to steward what God is calling us to, then we must build good foundations in ourselves and allow God to transform us.

When choosing people to manage the distribution of food in Acts, it says, *"Therefore, brothers, choose from among you seven men with good reputations [men of godly character and moral integrity], full of the Spirit and of wisdom, whom we may put in charge of this task."* (Acts 6:3, AMP)

The Bible talks about appointing elders and deacons (leadership), in 1 Timothy chapter 3, and lists the qualifications for such roles, some of which are: blameless and above reproach, self-controlled, hospitable, gentle and considerate, financially ethical, spiritually mature and many more.

While the process of building character may be uncomfortable and sometimes even painful at times, it's important to grow through this process.

Empowered IN HIM Workbook

Like I mentioned in the first chapter, we cannot teach something that we have not learnt, we cannot lead someone where we haven't been, we cannot give what we haven't got.

Being planted in a church where you can grow and develop your gift is essential. This means you have a local church family with leadership you submit to and who are covering you and praying for you, to whom you are accountable, and where you serve so that you can grow. The Bible says *"Those who are planted in the house of the Lord shall flourish in the courts of our God."* (Psalms 92:13 NKJV)

By being committed and serving in a local church we will grow in character, in maturity, in understanding, in faith, in wisdom, in self-discipline and so much more! By being planted we can be trained and equipped, be protected spiritually and have the opportunity to share and practice our gifts in a safe space. All these elements will help to develop the character in you that is needed to "cradle the call".

Jesus speaks of pruning in John, *"Every branch in Me that does not bear fruit He takes away; and every branch that bears fruit He prunes, that it may bear more fruit."* (John 15:2)

> *IN THE PROCESS OF PRUNING,*
> *GOD STRENGTHENS OUR FAITH*
> *AND DRAWS US CLOSER TO HIMSELF.*

If we allow the process and the pruning, through tests and trials, through loss or disappointment, through confronting and dealing with sin in our own lives, our character will be developed and we will display the fruit of the spirit without which we cannot operate in the gifts of the spirit.

"But the fruit of the Spirit is love, joy, peace, longsuffering, kindness, goodness, faithfulness, gentleness, self-control. Against such there is no law. And those who are Christ's have crucified the flesh with its passions and desires. If we live in the Spirit, let us also walk in the Spirit." (Galatians 5:22-25)

Allow yourself to grow; don't bypass the tests and trials, the results of which are proven character, completely mature, lacking nothing!

James 1:2-4 (AMP) says,
"Consider it nothing but joy, my brothers and sisters, whenever you fall into various trials. Be assured that the testing of your faith [through experience] produces endurance [leading to spiritual maturity, and inner peace]. And let endurance have its perfect result and do a thorough work, so that you may be perfect and completely developed [in your faith], lacking in nothing."

And this scripture, Romans 5:3-4 (AMP),
"And not only this, but [with joy] let us exult in our sufferings and rejoice in our hardships, knowing that hardship (distress, pressure, trouble) produces patient endurance; and endurance, proven character (spiritual maturity); and proven character, hope and confident assurance [of eternal salvation]."

Have vision/set goals
The Bible says, *"Without a vision, the people perish"*, (Proverbs 29:18).

It is important to have vision and to set goals. We don't go from salvation to apostle overnight! We need to become trained and equipped, to develop our gifts and talents.

Why is vision important?
- *Vision gives direction*
- *Vision prevents mistakes*
- *Vision avoids wasting resources*
- *Vision gives purpose*
- *Vision provides motivation*
- *Vision aligns and prioritises goals*

Habakkuk 2:2, *"Then the Lord answered me and said: "Write the vision And make it plain on tablets, That he may run who reads it."*

Without vision we drift, but with vision we unite with Gods plan, with others and press forward towards all He has for us.

"Not that I have already attained, or am already perfected; but I press on, that I may lay hold of that for which Christ Jesus has also laid hold of me. Brethren, I do not count myself to have apprehended; but one thing I do, forgetting those things which are behind and reaching forward to those things which are ahead, I press toward the goal for the prize of the upward call of God in Christ Jesus." (Philippians 3:12-14 NKJV)

Get a heavenly perspective and set Kingdom-based goals. Sit with the Lord and listen to His voice. Proverbs 3:5-6 says, *"Trust in the Lord with all your heart, And lean not on your own understanding; In all your ways acknowledge Him, And He shall direct your paths."*

Setting goals is like a map that leads you to your God-given purpose and assignment; without it we could be wandering around in circles. Oftentimes people receive a prophetic word and then just sit and wait for it to come to pass. We need to take action!

It's not usual to receive a step-by- step plan from God on how to get from 'A' to 'B'. The process is about building our faith on the way, developing trust in the One who is leading us, teaching us to listen to His voice.

Ultimately, the more time we spend with Him, the more we hear His heart and follow His lead. Set smaller goals, look for the open doors, follow the peace that far exceeds our understanding.

LEAN INTO HIM, FIX YOUR GAZE ON HIM;
THE JOURNEY IS NOT ALWAYS EASY,
*BUT IT IS **SO** WORTH IT!*

WE CANNOT LEAD SOMEONE WHERE WE HAVEN'T BEEN, WE CANNOT GIVE WHAT WE HAVEN'T GOT.

Questions

What are some areas that you need to build your character?

_____
_____
_____
_____
_____
_____
_____
_____
_____
_____
_____
_____
_____
_____

Who are your leaders/mentors that you are submitted to?

_____
_____
_____
_____
_____
_____
_____
_____
_____
_____
_____
_____
_____

Where do you see yourself in one year? In five years? In twenty years? (Should the Lord tarry)

What steps are you putting in place to reach these dreams?

_____
_____
_____
_____
_____
_____
_____
_____
_____
_____
_____
_____
_____
_____
_____
_____
_____
_____
_____
_____
_____
_____
_____
_____
_____

Reflection

If you don't have a mentor, ask the Lord to show you who He would like you to partner with and be accountable to.

Reflection

Reflection

Additional Notes

Additional Notes

Empowered IN HIM Workbook

Additional Notes

Additional Notes

Additional Notes

Additional Notes

Additional Notes

Additional Notes

Additional Notes

Additional Notes

www.ingramcontent.com/pod-product-compliance
Lightning Source LLC
Chambersburg PA
CBHW061814290426
44110CB00026B/2866